My Book

A MUE

MARY BETY

Stardust
Book of
Prayers

Illustrations by
Stina Nagel

Stardust
Books

THE C. R. GIBSON COMPANY
Publishers
NORWALK, CONNECTICUT

Lord, teach a little child to pray,
And, oh, accept my prayer;
Thou canst hear all the words I say,
For Thou art everywhere.
A little sparrow cannot fall,
Unnoticed, Lord, by Thee;
And though I am so young and small,
Thou canst take care of me.

Now I wake and see the light,
Thy love was with me through the night;
To Thee I speak again and pray
That Thou wilt lead me all the day.
I ask not for myself alone,
But for Thy children, every one.

Keep my little tongue today.
Keep me gentle while I play.
Keep my hands from doing wrong.
Keep my feet the whole day long.
Keep me all, O Jesus mild,
Keep me ever Thy dear child.

Heavenly Father, hear our prayer.
Keep us in Thy loving care.
Guard us through the livelong day
In our work and in our play.
Keep us pure and strong and true,
In everything we say and do.

For flowers that bloom about our feet,
    Father, we thank Thee.
For tender grass so fresh and sweet,
    Father, we thank Thee.
For the song of bird and hum of bee,
For all things fair we hear or see,
Father in heaven, we thank Thee.

For blue of stream and blue of sky,
    Father, we thank Thee.
For pleasant shade of branches high,
    Father, we thank Thee.
For fragrant air and cooling breeze,
For beauty of the blooming trees,
Father in heaven, we thank Thee.

Thank You, God, for feet to run,
Thank You for my play and fun;
For eyes to see, for hands to lift,
For food to eat, and every gift
That makes me strong and wish to sing,
"Thank You, God, for everything."

O God, I ask Thee to forgive,
Help me the better way to live.
Make me stronger to do right.
Help me try with all my might.
So many things are hard to do;
O keep me, Father, strong and true.

Jesus, keep me all this day,
When at school and when at play;
Help me love and trust in Thee,
From all evil keep me free.

Father, we thank Thee for the night
And for the pleasant morning light,
For rest, and food, and loving care,
And all that makes the day so fair.

Help us to do the things we should,
To be to others kind and good,
In all we do, in work and play,
To love Thee better every day.

Father, keep me all day long
From all hurtful things and wrong;
Make me thine obedient child,
Make me loving, gentle, mild.

Lord, bless my playmates, this I pray;
Bless us together while we play;
Bless us apart, and make us know
Thy love, wherever we may go.

All this day Thy hand has led me,
And I thank Thee for Thy care.
Thou hast clothed me, warmed and fed me;
Blessed Jesus, hear my prayer.

Be near me, Lord Jesus,
I ask Thee to stay
Close by me forever
And love me, I pray.

Jesus, tender Shepherd, hear me:
Bless Thy little child tonight;
Through the darkness be Thou near me;
Keep me safe till morning light.

Now that light has gone away;
Saviour, listen while I pray,
Asking Thee to watch and keep
And to send me quiet sleep.
Jesus, Saviour, wash away
All that has been wrong today;
Help me every day to be
Good and gentle, more like Thee.

Now I lay me down to sleep;
I pray Thee, Lord, my soul to keep.
Guide me through the starry night
And wake me when the sun shines bright.

The Doxology

Praise God, from whom all blessings flow;
Praise Him, all creatures here below;
Praise Him above, ye heavenly host:
Praise Father, Son, and Holy Ghost.

Amen.

Thank You for the world so sweet,
Thank You for the food we eat,
Thank You for the birds that sing,
Thank You, God, for everything.

Thou art great and Thou art good,
And we thank Thee for this food,
By Thy hand must all be fed;
Give us, Lord, our daily bread.

For health and food, for love and friends,
For everything Thy goodness sends.
Father in heaven, we thank Thee so
For countless blessings here below.

God bless all those that I love:
God bless all those that love me;
God bless all those that love
those that I love,
And all those that love those
that love me.

Our thanks to Thee, our God most high,
Thou dost our every need supply.

Amen.

Thank You, dear God, for the beautiful day,
For home and for care and for happy play.
Thank You, for rest when the day is done,
And love that takes care of us, every one.